Original title:
The Enigma Express

Copyright © 2024 Creative Arts Management OÜ
All rights reserved.

Author: Zachary Prescott
ISBN HARDBACK: 978-9916-90-314-8
ISBN PAPERBACK: 978-9916-90-315-5

Passengers of the Mysterious Route

On a train where whispers dwell,
Secrets ride like tales to tell.
Windows frame the hazy light,
Echoes murmur through the night.

Faces fade, yet eyes remain,
Each a story, joy or pain.
Time stretches on this winding track,
No turning back, no looking back.

Railways of Intrigue and Wonder

Beneath the stars, the rails do gleam,
A ribbon of dreams, a silver stream.
Tracks lead on, through shadowed trees,
With a hint of magic in the breeze.

Whistle blows, the journey starts,
Fueling hopes and daring hearts.
Curved horizons, secrets unfurl,
In this traveler's enchanting world.

Ghosts in the Sleeping Compartments

Silent specters haunt the space,
Memories drift, leave not a trace.
Each compartment holds a tale,
Of love and loss, a wistful wail.

Pillow soft where dreams once grew,
Blankets sing of those who knew.
In the quiet, whispers flow,
From the past, where shadows glow.

All Aboard the Questioning Express

Tickets punched with hopes unknown,
Questions rise like seeds once sown.
As the wheels turn, thoughts collide,
In this journey, none can hide.

Who am I in this fleeting space?
What is time in this endless race?
Answers hidden in the night,
All aboard, seek the light.

Journey Through the Veiled Fog

Shadows dance in muted light,
Whispers call from depths of night.
Footsteps lost on winding trails,
Silent stories, breathless tales.

Misty veils stretch far and wide,
Guiding souls that seek to hide.
Through the fog, the heartbeats pound,
In the stillness, truths are found.

Tickets to the Unseen

In pockets deep, the secrets lie,
Illusions held where shadows fly.
Each ticket grants a glimpse, a view,
Of worlds where dreams are born anew.

Through the gates of hope we tread,
With every step, old fears we shed.
The unseen beckons with a smile,
Whisking us away for a while.

Conundrums on the Rolling Rails

Wheels rattle on the iron way,
Questions rise with light of day.
Tracks that twist and turn in quest,
Reveal the minds that never rest.

Voices blend in rhythmic flow,
Puzzles form in undertow.
Each stop a chance to pause and think,
Before the train's next daring clink.

The Silent Train of Forgotten Dreams

In shadows sleeps a train long still,
Carrying hopes that time won't kill.
With each breath, the memories sigh,
Echoes of laughter drift on high.

Rusty wheels and faded tracks,
Hold the stories life unpacks.
In silent cars, the wishes gleam,
A gentle chase of a lost dream.

Illusions on the Expressway

Mirages flicker in the heat,
Concrete jungles at our feet.
Cars rush by like fleeting dreams,
Reality unravels at the seams.

A distant sun, a shadow's dance,
In every glance, a second chance.
Life rushes past with a hollow sound,
In these illusions, we're lost, not found.

The asphalt stretches, tales untold,
Whispers linger, secrets unfold.
Every curve conceals a truth,
Speeding toward an endless youth.

Beyond the Veil of the Horizon

Where colors merge in twilight's glow,
A canvas broad, a world to flow.
Beyond the veil, what lies in wait?
A journey's end or a new fate?

Clouds embrace the setting sun,
Whispers of dreams, just begun.
Fields of gold stretch far and wide,
In the dusk, the stars collide.

Mountains high, where eagles soar,
An echo stirs on distant shore.
With every step, the unknown calls,
Beyond the veil, the heart enthralls.

Mysteries on the Midnight Train

Rails that hum with secrets deep,
As shadows glide, the lost ones weep.
A train of thoughts, both dark and bright,
Chasing phantoms into the night.

Windows fogged, reflections swirl,
A world unknown begins to unfurl.
Each car a story, whispered low,
In the silence, dreams overflow.

Through tunnels dark, the heart will race,
Finding echoes in a timeless space.
Mysteries linger, cloaked in air,
On this midnight train, we share our care.

Whispers of the Wandering Carriage

A carriage rolls through fields of green,
Carried by tales yet unseen.
Whispers dance on the gentle breeze,
Fables drift like autumn leaves.

Horses trot with rhythmic grace,
Each hoofbeat holds a secret place.
As daylight fades, shadows creep,
In wandering dreams, the heart will leap.

Moonlight glows on paths unknown,
The seeds of night are gently sown.
Every mile a story spun,
In the twilight, we become one.

The Cryptic Conductor's Call

In shadows deep where silence waits,
A conductor's voice calls through the gates.
With secrets held in whispered tones,
The path ahead is carved in bones.

His lantern shines on tracks unseen,
Echoes linger, where have they been?
Each note a thread, a woven fate,
A journey strange, we contemplate.

Tracks of Uncertainty

Along the rails where no one goes,
Footsteps fade in the mist that grows.
Each station stops with whispered fear,
The tracks of time, so vague and sheer.

A puzzle laid with every mile,
In uncertainty, we search and smile.
What tales emerge from rusted seams?
The future dances in our dreams.

Wanderlust and Whispers

The heart is drawn to distant lands,
With wanderlust that softly stands.
Whispers ride upon the breeze,
Stories carried from beyond the trees.

Each journey starts with a quiet call,
A nudge to seek, to rise, to fall.
Where roads converge and shadows meet,
Adventure beckons on nimble feet.

Bizarre Encounters in Transit

Upon the train, strange faces gleam,
Every glance a fleeting dream.
The man with fire in his eyes,
Speaks of wonders veiled in skies.

A woman laughs with tales absurd,
Words like puzzles, seldom heard.
In transit, life feels unfamiliar,
Each encounter, a tale peculiar.

Hidden Compositions of the Steel Symphony

In shadows deep, the notes arise,
Whispers of metal, under darkened skies.
Strings of fate in silence play,
Echoes of dreams that drift away.

Beneath the rust, a song concealed,
In every crack, emotions revealed.
Harmonies forged in fire and steel,
Crafting the wounds that time will heal.

Train of Thought through Foggy Nights

Through misty trails, the engine roars,
Thoughts like carriages on open shores.
Each stop a memory, blurred and bright,
Journeying softly into the night.

Voices murmur in the shrouded air,
A whispered truth found here and there.
Lurking doubts rattle the frame,
Yet hope steers the course of the same.

Riddles through the Iron Veil

Beneath the surface, questions weave,
In twisted shadows, truth deceives.
Iron bars hold secrets tight,
Waiting for the break of light.

Each riddle etched in fleeting time,
A puzzle shaped in rust and grime.
Unlocking doors with nimble hands,
Finding answers in shifting sands.

Traces of the Unidentified Traveler

Footprints linger on the path of dust,
An unknown figure, in shadows, must.
What stories lie behind each step,
A tale of journeys, dreams adept?

Silhouettes haunt the fading light,
Ghosts of wanderers lost to night.
Maps unwritten guide their way,
In their silence, secrets stay.

Unmasking the Mystery of Distance

In shadows cast by years gone by,
A whisper rides the evening sky.
We count the miles, yet feel the pull,
Where silence reigns, and hearts are full.

Between the words left unsaid,
A tapestry of dreams is spread.
We search for meaning in the space,
Where love and longing interlace.

The stars may hide behind the veils,
Yet in their glow, hope never fails.
Across the chasms, we will strive,
To find the way, to feel alive.

The Unseen Passengers of Time

In the corners of our minds they linger,
With fragile dreams at the edge of fingers.
Each tick a moment, soft and shy,
Unfolding like a gentle sigh.

They weave through laughter, sorrow too,
In every heartbeat, old yet new.
Invisible friends that guide our feet,
On paths of fate where journeys meet.

Their stories etched in every gaze,
In fleeting glances, a quiet blaze.
The clock may turn, but they will stay,
Through every dusk, and every day.

Fables from the Forgotten Railway

Beneath the rust, old tales abide,
Of lives entwined where trains collide.
With whispers carried on the breeze,
And echoes held in ancient trees.

The lanterns glow, a guiding light,
For souls who wander through the night.
Each station holds a story's thread,
Of laughter shared, and tears long shed.

Through fields of gold and iron grey,
The past and present find their way.
A journey marked by love and loss,
In every heartbeat, there's a cost.

Veils of Fog and Steel

In morning mist, where shadows creep,
The world awakens from its sleep.
With breath of steel, the train does roar,
It sings of journeys, forevermore.

Veils of fog conceal the day,
As dreams arise and drift away.
Each clatter tells a tale of yore,
Where hopes take flight, and spirits soar.

Through tunnels dark and valleys wide,
Across the land, we will abide.
In veils of fog, our hearts reveal,
The strength within the love we feel.

Whispers of the Moving Shadows

In the dim light, shadows dance,
Whispers float in a ghostly trance.
Leaves rustle softly with the night,
Secrets hidden just out of sight.

The moon gazes down with a sigh,
Stars twinkle like secrets in the sky.
Footsteps trace paths in the dark,
Every echo leaves its mark.

Figures flit through the misty air,
Callings that linger everywhere.
Silhouettes weave tales untold,
In the twilight, the mysteries unfold.

As dawn breaks, whispers cease,
In the silence, there's a piece.
Of the stories told in the night,
Fading softly with morning light.

Secrets on the Iron Path

Beneath the rust of forgotten years,
An iron path whispers and hears.
Footfalls echo with tales of old,
In the crevices, secrets unfold.

Each rail a memory, each tie a clue,
Songs of journeys that once blew.
Night rides carry the dreams afar,
Guided softly by the evening star.

Trains roll by like wishes in flight,
Carrying shadows into the night.
The rumble speaks of lands unknown,
Hearts entwined where they have flown.

As daybreak warms the chilly air,
The path lays bare what it may share.
Stories linger in the morning dew,
Brightened by the sun's soft hue.

Enigmatic Journeys Through Twilight

Twilight drapes a shroud of grace,
Enigmas linger in this space.
Each path leads to a dreamer's heart,
Where reality and magic part.

Colors blend in a delicate swirl,
Mysteries beckon like a pearl.
Wanderers tread on this gentle seam,
Chasing shadows that softly gleam.

Voices whisper from yesteryear,
Calling softly, drawing near.
Journeys woven in twilight threads,
Map the journey where courage treads.

As night deepens, secrets unfurl,
Lost in a dream, the spirits whirl.
In each heartbeat lies a spark,
Guiding souls through the endless dark.

Curiosities in Midnight Cars

Cars glide silently through the dark,
Curiosities ignite the spark.
Windows down, the cool breeze flows,
In the quiet night, adventure grows.

Streetlights blink like winking eyes,
Secrets hidden beneath the skies.
Each turn taken, a chance embraced,
In the midnight, wheels are laced.

Stories shared in the backseat hum,
Echoes of laughter, the beat of drums.
Every mile unfolds a new tale,
As moonlight dances over each trail.

So let the road stretch wide and far,
In midnight cars, we chase a star.
With every journey, we learn and see,
The beauty found in mystery.

The Uncharted Path of Steel

Beneath the moon's soft gaze, they ride,
Through shadows deep, with dreams as guide.
The rails hum low, a tale untold,
Of journeys bold, through night so cold.

They travel lands that time forgot,
On tracks where silence weaves each thought.
The steel sings songs of paths unseen,
While whispers rise in twilight's sheen.

Ghosts of engines long laid bare,
Echo through the dusky air.
Each click and clack, a heartbeat's dance,
Unraveling fate with every chance.

With lantern light to show the way,
They forge ahead, come what may.
The uncharted path, a bold reveal,
In every mile, they dare to feel.

Time Travelers on the Local Line

A whistle blows, the engine starts,
With every stop, it moves our hearts.
In carriages where stories blend,
Time bends and sways, like old friends.

Passengers drift through epochs vast,
With echoes from the distant past.
Each station holds a whispered clue,
Of futures bright and shadows blue.

The scenery shifts with every mile,
History's pulse, a fleeting smile.
They watch the world from windows wide,
As timelines bend, and dreams collide.

Forever caught in transit's grace,
They change the past, in every space.
On local lines, where time entwines,
They weave their fates through shifting signs.

The Hidden Chronicles of Train Journeys

In whispered tales of steely might,
The trains unveil the stars at night.
Each track a chapter, each car a page,
Unfolding dreams of every age.

From bustling stations, stories rise,
Of hope and love, beneath the skies.
The hidden chronicles, a soft embrace,
Where time can warp and fears erase.

Over mountains, through valleys low,
The journey's heartbeat starts to flow.
With every mile, a secret shared,
In silence rich, their souls are bared.

So ride the rails, let go of time,
In every clang, a silent rhyme.
For every journey holds a spark,
Of hidden tales that leave their mark.

Midnight Whispers in Motion

As shadows dance on velvet ground,
The midnight train glides, soft profound.
With each vibration, dreams take flight,
In whispered tones beneath the night.

Through windows fogged with hidden fears,
The travelers share their silent tears.
With every turn, revelations bloom,
In darkened cars, where heartbeats loom.

The stars above a watchful choir,
As steel meets time in silent fire.
A journey woven through the dark,
Midnight whispers leave their mark.

So let the rails guide paths unknown,
In twilight's hush, we'll find our own.
For in the night, we rise and fall,
As midnight whispers call us all.

The Concealed Itinerary

In shadows deep, a map unfolds,
Whispers of journeys, stories untold.
Markers hidden, lost in the trees,
Guiding the seekers, carried by breeze.

Paths once traveled, now fade away,
Echoes of footsteps, where children would play.
With each turn taken, a mystery lies,
Under the starlit, uncharted skies.

Attractions of a Vanishing Trail

Beneath the canopy, colors collide,
Nature's canvas, a fleeting tide.
Footprints of time, where colors fade,
Memories linger, in shadows made.

Whispers of creatures that once roamed free,
Silence of secrets held tenderly.
Through brush and bramble, an echo remains,
The pulse of the earth, in soft, silent chains.

Secrets Stored in Old Carriages

Rusty wheels turn, vintage dreams,
Hushed tales linger in sunbeam streams.
Windows framed with a frosted hue,
Revealing glimpses of lives that flew.

Dusty corners hold laughter and sighs,
Beneath every seat, the past softly lies.
Carved initials tell stories of love,
Worn leather whispers of stars above.

Cryptic Crossings of the Iron Way

Tracks of steel, like veins in the night,
Railway whispers draw forth the light.
Crossings where destinies entwine,
In the rhythm of wheels, lives combine.

Signals flicker, a mystic dance,
Riders with dreams, lost in a trance.
Through tunnels dark, to futures unknown,
Journey unfolds on the seeds we've sown.

Chasing Ghosts on Gilded Tracks

Riding on whispers, we glide through the night,
Shadows whisper secrets in pale silver light.
Gilded tracks beckon, where memories entwine,
Chasing lost moments, their glow we define.

Footsteps like breezes, they fade in the mist,
Flickers of laughter, too fragile to persist.
The echoes of journeys, both distant and near,
In the heart of the railways, the phantoms appear.

Railways of the Arcane

A pull of the spirit, the train moves anew,
Mysteries linger where shadows accrue.
Carriages rattling, with tales yet untold,
Railways of arcane, their magic unfolds.

In tunnels of twilight, the past finds a way,
Beyond every heartbeat, the spirits will sway.
Navigating pathways where time bends and flows,
The journey's a spell that the night softly knows.

Haunting Echoes of the Whistle

The whistle rings out with a ghostly refrain,
Calling the lost souls to board the old train.
Each note a reminder of paths left behind,
Haunting echoes linger in the chambers of mind.

Onward we travel where shadows converge,
A symphony written, their voices emerge.
Whispers and wails in the cold air reside,
Reminders of journeys the heart cannot hide.

Shadows Beneath the Carriage

Underneath the carriage, where daylight won't reach,
Shadows hum softly, their lessons to teach.
With every faint rattle, a story unfolds,
Whispers of travelers, both timid and bold.

Secrets shared quietly, beneath rickety beams,
Carried along on the pulse of our dreams.
We linger in twilight, where echoes collide,
In shadows, we find both our fear and our pride.

Tracks and Tranquility of Thought

In quiet woods the train does glide,
A gentle whisper through the trees.
Thoughts meander, calm inside,
Carried softly, like the breeze.

To follow tracks where dreams do flow,
Each moment savored, pure delight.
The path reveals what we don't know,
As stars embrace the cloak of night.

In shadows cast, reflections bloom,
The heart finds peace in soft retreat.
Within the mind, within the room,
Clarity and chaos meet.

Past fields of gold and rivers wide,
The journey whispers tales untold.
Tracks of wisdom softly guide,
Through tranquil thoughts, we bid the bold.

Puzzles on a Stormy Night

Lightning paints the night in white,
A puzzle formed from dark and light.
Rain taps softly on the glass,
Each drop a question, moments pass.

Thunder rumbles, thoughts collide,
What secrets in the storm do hide?
The wind a riddle, fierce and strong,
It sings a haunting, wild song.

In shadows deep, the answers sway,
Each flash unveils a game to play.
The heart races, the mind takes flight,
Solving puzzles through the night.

With every crash, a challenge calls,
While darkness wraps and silence falls.
Beneath the chaos, stillness sighs,
In every storm, a truth replies.

Echoes Amidst the Iron Wilderness

In steel and stone, where shadows creep,
The echoes of a past run deep.
Forgotten tales in rust reside,
A wilderness where dreams collide.

The howl of wind through iron bends,
Retells the stories of lost friends.
With every cry, a memory breaks,
In whispered winds, the silence wakes.

Graffiti dreams on aged concrete,
The city breathes, no chance to sleep.
Through tangled paths of heart and soul,
The echoes guide, and make us whole.

Among the ruins, hope still thrives,
In every crack, the spirit strives.
Embrace the noise, the life's refrain,
In wilderness, let hearts remain.

The Labyrinth of the Tracks

A winding path of dreams and doubts,
The railway sings its ancient song.
Curving round with twists and shouts,
In the labyrinth, we all belong.

From station platforms, stories rise,
Whispers of journeys far away.
The tracks extend, beneath the skies,
Inviting souls to roam and play.

Each crossing holds a choice to make,
To follow or to turn aside.
In every choice, the hearts will ache,
As we journey with the tide.

In the complexity of paths we tread,
The labyrinth beckons, a dance of fate.
With hope we wander, not misled,
For each new turn leads to create.

Passengers in Paradox

Two roads diverge in twilight's glow,
Each one beckons, neither slow.
Choices linger, a dance in time,
A fleeting moment, fate's own rhyme.

We ride the waves of what could be,
Holding dreams as we journey free.
Yet shadows whisper of the path,
Behind us gleam the echoes' wrath.

Endless highways, endless skies,
A compass spinning, the heart replies.
In paradox, our spirits soar,
Forever seeking, forever more.

Whispers of Lost Destinations

The map is torn, the ink has faded,
Yet still we travel, unafraid and jaded.
Each step we take, the past unfolds,
In whispers soft, its story told.

Silent echoes of places once known,
In every corner, the seeds are sown.
Ghostly figures in twilight's embrace,
Leading us forward through time and space.

Roads forgotten, yet never lost,
Each winding turn reveals the cost.
We seek but find what cannot be grasped,
In echoes of dreams, our futures clasped.

The Cryptic Journey Ahead

A map of riddles in hand we hold,
Paths obscured, stories untold.
Curiosity drives us through the night,
In search of the dawn, a glimmering light.

Mysteries beckon, the air is thick,
With whispers of fate, both gentle and quick.
Every turn a new tale to spin,
As we stand on the edge, ready to begin.

Mountains loom in the distance still,
Their peaks echoing a dauntless thrill.
What lies beyond the veil so thin?
The cryptic journey, let it begin.

Memories on the Windshield

Raindrops trace on a glassy pane,
In every streak, there's joy and pain.
Faded pictures of faces dear,
Stirring echoes of laughter and tears.

The road ahead reflects the past,
In fleeting moments, shadows cast.
With every mile, the tales arise,
From whispered dreams to soft goodbyes.

The engine hums a lullaby sweet,
Memories dance in the rhythm of beat.
Through every curve, through every bend,
We ride as time begins to blend.

The Last Station of Secrets

In shadows deep, where whispers dwell,
The last train rolls, its stories swell.
Ghostly echoes of laughter, lost in time,
Secrets hidden beneath the grime.

A flickering light, a vacant stare,
Memories trapped in the midnight air.
The clock strikes twelve, the end of the line,
Promises fractured, love's last sign.

Luggage forgotten, dreams laid bare,
Silent travelers, caught in despair.
A journey's end, yet questions remain,
What was once joy, now laced with pain.

So linger here, where the secrets hide,
In the last station, no place to bide.
For every heart that dares to roam,
Will find that silence calls us home.

Tracks Less Travelled

On winding paths where few have tread,
Lies a haven where dreams are bred.
Rusty rails and wildflowers bloom,
In the quiet, they echo the gloom.

Footsteps soft on the dusty way,
Whispers of night, come out to play.
Each mile a story, each turn a chance,
To dance with fate in a timeless trance.

Twilight paints the world in gold,
Tales of adventure, waiting to be told.
Through the thickets, fears abrade,
In the heart of the wild, memories fade.

Tracks less travelled, a glimpse of light,
Leading us home, through the night.
With every heartbeat, a new refrain,
In hidden paths, we lose our pain.

A Journey into the Heart of Mystery

Beneath the starlit, candle glow,
Secrets unfold, and feelings flow.
Echoes whisper from deep within,
Inviting us where the dreams begin.

Maps forgotten in the sands of time,
Each step forward feels like a rhyme.
Guided by stars, with spirits bold,
A journey awaits, more precious than gold.

Labyrinths twist in shadows play,
The heart beats loud, then fades away.
In the silence, we confront our fear,
And find the truth that draws us near.

With every breath, we venture forth,
To the heart of mystery, a hidden worth.
For in the unknown, magic thrives,
In the journey's depths, true love survives.

Whispers Beneath the Sapphire Sky

Underneath a vast sapphire night,
Whispers flutter like stars in flight.
Each breeze carries a tale untold,
Of love, of loss, and dreams of old.

The moon refracts a silver gleam,
Caressing the earth with a gentle beam.
In hushed tones, the cosmos sings,
Of hope reborn, and the joy it brings.

Clouds drift softly, like thoughts unbound,
While passion's pulse reverberates around.
In each heartbeat, connections flare,
As we find solace in the night air.

So listen closely, let your heart fly,
For magic lives beneath the sky.
In the realm of whispers, spirits soar,
And remind us what we're searching for.

Lost Connections on the Iron Trail

Tracks twist and turn in the mist,
Whispers linger, dreams persist.
Memories scatter like leaves on stone,
Hearts once together, now stand alone.

Steel giants tread with a mournful sound,
Bridges echo stories long unbound.
Faces forgotten in shades of gray,
Time slips away, fades to dismay.

Rusting relics of journeys passed,
Chasing shadows, the die is cast.
Voices echo through the empty cars,
Lost connections, like distant stars.

In the silence of twilight's embrace,
Lies the ache of a forsaken place.
Each rail a thread to what once was whole,
A longing journey, a fractured soul.

Enigmas Beneath the Cloaked Stars

In night's velvet cloak, mysteries weave,
Stars are secrets, beg to believe.
Whispers of worlds in the cosmic dance,
In the silence, every glance a chance.

Galaxies spin tales of old,
Silverlining dreams, manifold gold.
Constellations speak in riddles rare,
Eyes turned upward, hearts laid bare.

Lurking shadows in the vast unknown,
Questions linger, truth overgrown.
Beneath the glitter, lies dark and light,
Enigmas whisper through the night.

A journey inward, a quest for grace,
Each star a beacon in time and space.
In the dark, the answers lie,
Under the heavens, we seek the why.

A Train to Unravel the Unfathomable

On iron tracks, the train departs,
Churning dreams and restless hearts.
Each clack and clang, a tale unfurled,
A passage through this hidden world.

Windows frame the passing scenes,
Life unfolds in varied memes.
Voices echo, stories blend,
Every journey leads to the end.

Mysteries grasped but hard to hold,
Unfathomable truths, whispers bold.
Crossing valleys, a fleeting glance,
Time and space, an endless dance.

The wheels hum softly, a soothing song,
As we traverse where we belong.
With every mile, layers peel away,
In the night, the shadows play.

The Journey through Cryptic Landscapes

Through shadows deep, the path winds tight,
Every turn cloaked in twilight's light.
Mountains loom with secrets wide,
Mystic whispers, fate and pride.

Valleys echo tales untold,
Nature's canvas, vibrant and bold.
Hidden realms in the silence reign,
Each step forward, a lingering pain.

Clouds roll by, painting the skies,
Eyes searching for the truth in lies.
Deserts stretch with a longing sigh,
Where dreams are born and hopes can die.

In this journey, we seek and roam,
Finding pieces to build our home.
Through cryptic lands, we wander far,
In every heart beats a guiding star.

The Railroad of Uncertainty

Tracks stretch far, unseen ahead,
Whispers of doubt weave through my head.
Each mile a question, each turn a fate,
Traveling onward, but never quite late.

Beneath the sky, the stars align,
Guiding my thoughts along the spine.
Journeys begin with a single breath,
Between hopes of life and the shadow of death.

A train of doubts, it pulls me near,
Fueling the fire of my greatest fear.
Yet in the darkness, light flickers low,
Faith in the whispers, the winds that blow.

Unraveled thoughts, like ribbons in air,
A tapestry woven with dreams and despair.
The journey continues, no end in sight,
On this railroad of uncertainty, I ride through the night.

Journeys Beyond the Known Line

Beyond the horizon, where dreams collide,
Lies a path untouched, where secrets hide.
A journey beckons, enticing and bold,
With stories of wonder yet to be told.

Each step taken, a world to explore,
Mountains of courage, valleys of lore.
With every breath, a thread unwinds,
Weaving the fabric of open minds.

Beyond the maps, in lands unknown,
In every moment, a seed is sown.
Connections are forged, where hearts align,
As we traverse these journeys, beyond the known line.

Turning the page, we step into light,
Embracing the shadows, embracing the night.
For every journey starts with a single sign,
And leads us to places our spirits can shine.

Steam and Shadows Intertwined

Puffs of steam rise in the twilight glow,
Shadows dancing, where the wild winds blow.
The engine thunders, a heartbeat strong,
In the melody of night, I find my song.

Ties that bind in the vapors of time,
Symbols of journeys in rhythm and rhyme.
Every twist and turn, a tale to spin,
Where shadows lie deep, and dreams begin.

Tracks converge, like paths of the heart,
In the steam and shadows, we're never apart.
Each whistle calls, like a lover's plea,
Inviting our souls to roam wild and free.

Embrace the night, let the echoes sing,
In the realm of the lost, my spirit takes wing.
For as long as there's steam, and shadows entwined,
The essence of travel will always remind.

The Corridor of Questions

In a corridor lit by flickering light,
Questions linger, woven through night.
What lies ahead in the realms unseen?
Sparks of curiosity, vibrant and keen.

Whispers of answers, elusive and shy,
Navigating paths where the echoes fly.
In every heartbeat, a quest ignites,
Finding the courage in small, quiet fights.

Doors line the hallway, each one a choice,
Yet silence speaks louder, it calls with a voice.
With a key of wonder, I push through the door,
Unlocking the mysteries longing to soar.

So hand in hand, let's tread with grace,
In the corridor of questions, we find our place.
For with each inquiry, we unravel the night,
Awakening dreams, embracing the light.

The Forgotten Stops

In the shadows where old tracks lie,
Whispers of journeys float on by.
Rusty signs tell stories untold,
Of dreams and hopes that once were bold.

Deserted platforms, silence reigns,
Echoes linger, like soft refrains.
Each corner hides a secret past,
Forgotten places, memories cast.

Moss-covered benches, time forgot,
Ghostly figures in thought-filled spots.
Waiting for trains that never came,
Their journeys lost, yet still we claim.

What lies beyond the faded trails?
Adventures marked by winds and gales.
In quiet nights, their tales emerge,
The forgotten stops, where dreams converge.

Timeless Adventures on Steel

Clattering wheels on iron veins,
The pulse of travel, freedom gains.
Through valleys deep and mountains high,
On endless tracks beneath the sky.

Whistle cries signal the embark,
A journey brighter than a spark.
Together, all our hearts ignite,
As stars above begin to light.

With every mile, we find our way,
In every sunset, night and day.
Stories woven on steel so fine,
Timeless adventures, yours and mine.

Through tunnels dark, and rivers wide,
The rails our compass, our guide.
Onward we ride, with spirits free,
In the heart of the train, we're meant to be.

Mysteries of the Midnight Locomotive

Midnight whispers, shadows creep,
Beneath the stars, we lose our sleep.
The locomotive, fierce and grand,
Guides us through this magical land.

Whirling lights like fleeting dreams,
Carving paths through silver streams.
What mysteries lie in the night?
In every chug, a spark of light.

An old conductor with tales to share,
Of ghostly passengers and midnight air.
Riddles linger, hearts entwine,
In the echoes of the trains that shine.

Each stop a portal to the unknown,
Revealing secrets we've never shown.
In the nocturnal dance, we find our tune,
With the midnight locomotive, under the moon.

Serpentine Stories of the Night

Winding tracks like tales unsaid,
Serpentine journeys where dreams are bred.
Through moonlit valleys, shadows twine,
In every curve, a sip of wine.

An old whistle calls, a beckoning tune,
Guiding our hearts beneath the moon.
Where the horizon kisses the sky,
We ride the waves, we soar and fly.

The night unfolds with whispered sighs,
Beneath the canvas of starlit skies.
Every turn reveals a sight,
In serpentine stories of pure delight.

With every mile, our spirits swell,
In the arms of night, we weave our spell.
So let us wander, let us roam,
In the tales we tell, we find our home.

Portals of the Unfathomable

Through shadows deep, the portals rise,
Ancient whispers fill the skies.
Gates to realms where dreams take flight,
Lost in time, we chase the light.

In silent woods, the echoes call,
Mystic paths where phantoms crawl.
Each step closer, borders blur,
In the heart of night, we stir.

Beneath the stars, we seek the truth,
Faded memories of our youth.
With every breath, the secrets surge,
Together in this timeless urge.

Through portals wide, we dare to leap,
Into the unknown, shadows creep.
Hand in hand, we'll find our way,
In the unfathomable, we'll stay.

A Ticket to the Encrypted

Hidden paths with clues abound,
In whispers low, truths can be found.
A ticket drawn from shadows wide,
Unlocks the door where secrets hide.

In cryptic runes, our fate is cast,
Every moment shared, a bond unsurpassed.
The journey starts with a single key,
To worlds unknown, just you and me.

Between the lines, the whispers speak,
Of dreams awakened, of hearts that seek.
As stars appear, the answers glow,
In encrypted words, we come to know.

With every step, we break the code,
As journeys weave through the enigmas bestowed.
Together we forge, a story untamed,
A ticket to memories, forever named.

Journey Through Veiled Landscapes

In veils of mist, the landscapes sway,
Guided by stars, we wander away.
Each horizon hides a tale untold,
Mysteries wrapped in the night's soft hold.

Through valleys deep and mountains steep,
Whispers of history lull us to sleep.
Where shadows dance and sunlight beams,
Our hearts align with forgotten dreams.

Time sheds its skin, a river flows,
In veiled landscapes, our purpose grows.
Together we roam where spirits glide,
In the tapestry of twilight, we bide.

With every turn, the journey expands,
Veiled vistas held in life's tender hands.
In the quiet depths, we find our place,
In the journey's embrace, we trust, we trace.

Secrets of the Silver Track

Upon the silver track we tread,
With ancient whispers in our head.
Each step reveals a story's thread,
Of paths unwalked and dreams unsaid.

Under the moon's soft, glimmering gaze,
We wander through a shimmering haze.
The secrets lie just out of sight,
In shadows deep as day turns night.

Every moment feels like time's embrace,
In the quiet turns, we find our place.
Leaving behind the weight of the past,
On this silver track, hope is cast.

As stars align, our hearts will soar,
In secrets shared, forevermore.
On this journey, hand in hand we'll stand,
For the silver track leads to wonderland.

Timeless Journeys on Forgotten Routes

In whispers of the ancient paths,
Lost travelers tread on tales of yore,
Each footfall echoes, memories last,
As shadows dance on time's weathered shore.

Beneath the boughs of towering trees,
Lies a story no longer told,
Where the breeze hums forgotten keys,
To unlock secrets in sunlight's gold.

From cobblestones to dusty trails,
Adventures linger, dreams collide,
In every heartbeat, time unveils,
A journey where the past confides.

So wander on, let your soul ignite,
Through winding roads that twist and weave,
For in lost routes, there lies delight,
In timeless journeys, hearts believe.

The Hidden Mileposts of Memory

Markers stand where moments pause,
Eroded by time, yet bold in stance,
They whisper softly of life's cause,
In silent echoes, past's romance.

With every step, we search for signs,
Old photographs and faded trails,
Within the heart, a thread that twines,
The hidden mileposts tell our tales.

Underneath the stars so bright,
Stories linger in the shadows,
A compass spun by dreams' own light,
Guides us through the quiet meadows.

So treasure each small, forgotten mile,
For memories ride on fleeting winds,
In hidden posts, we find our smile,
As life's journey gently rescinds.

The Unsung Stories of Iron Wheels

Iron wheels that grind and groan,
Traversing tracks through night and day,
Each clank and scrape a tale alone,
Of journeys made along their way.

Through valleys deep and mountains high,
They roll with strength, yet quietly plead,
To recount the lives they pass by,
In murmurs shared, in dreams they feed.

Forgotten towns and whispering trains,
Carrying hopes and heavy loads,
Bearing witness to joy and pains,
In iron hearts, the story codes.

So let us listen, heed their call,
For in their journey, we find our place,
The unsung stories, narrated all,
By iron wheels in time's embrace.

Chronicles from the Rolling Obscurity

In rolling hills where shadows play,
Chapters of history unfold,
With every curve, a new ballet,
Stories hidden, waiting to be told.

Through quiet lanes, we drift away,
Where time stands still in twilight's glow,
Chronicles dressed in dusk's soft ray,
In whispers of the winds that flow.

Each corner turned, a glimpse of skies,
Unfurls the past, entwined with dreams,
In rolling obscurity, truth lies,
Revealed through memory's gentle seams.

So venture forth, let curiosity lead,
For every journey whispers a tale,
In the chronicles of life, we feed,
Collecting fragments where echoes sail.

Secrets Beneath the Steel Tracks

Whispers of forgotten dreams,
Lurking in the shadows deep,
Rusty bolts and weathered seams,
Guard the promises we keep.

Footsteps echo in the night,
Stories woven in the air,
Trains have witnessed every plight,
Secrets held without a care.

Muffled voices, long ago,
Drift between the iron ties,
Carried forth where shadows flow,
Beneath the stars, the truth lies.

What tales sleep beneath this ground?
What lovers' hopes and dreams reside?
In silence, memories abound,
As time and tracks begin to slide.

Echoes of an Unknown Journey

In twilight's glow, a train departs,
Wheels turn softly on the rails,
Every mile, it mends broken hearts,
Tales unfold and whisper tales.

Destinations lost to time,
A wanderer seeks solace here,
Each station holds a silent rhyme,
Where destinies collide and veer.

Voices murmur from afar,
As shadows blend with fading light,
Hopes arise like evening stars,
In darkness—with dreams taking flight.

The journey knows no end in sight,
A canvas stretched, a story's thread,
With echoes dancing in the night,
A path to travel, visions spread.

Shadows on the Passenger Line

Moonlight glimmers on the tracks,
Pacing memories through the haze,
Figures flicker, never slack,
In the quiet, lost in gaze.

Trains collide with dusk's embrace,
Carrying hopes on paper wings,
Every face—a fleeting trace,
Of lives entwined, of hidden things.

Ghostly whispers fill the air,
Riding smooth on steel's soft breath,
Caught within the endless stare,
Of passengers who rise from death.

Shadows dance where stories weave,
Among the echoes, soft and low,
In each moment, we believe,
The journeys interlace and flow.

Unraveled Tales of the Iron Horse

The iron horse begins to roar,
Its journey tells of ages past,
With every lurch, it craves for more,
Through valleys wide, its shadows cast.

Old stories clank on metal frames,
Wisps of laughter, love, and pain,
In every car, the spirit claims,
A traveler's heart, forever lain.

Journeying through the silent night,
Memories echo, soft and bright,
A tapestry of wrong and right,
As wheels unwind and sparks ignite.

The tracks remember each embrace,
The fleeting time, the tender glance,
In every bend, we find our place,
Along the iron's timeless dance.

Farewells of the Enigmatic Voyager

Upon the edge of dawn, he stands,
A traveler lost in distant lands.
With whispers soft, the wind does sway,
A silent promise to drift away.

His eyes hold tales of skies unknown,
Of fleeting moments, seeds he's sown.
Each step he takes, a heavy heart,
In every journey, worlds depart.

The sun sets low on paths untread,
While shadows lengthen, softly spread.
In every goodbye, a mystery brews,
A wanderer's soul, ever to choose.

Into the night, he disappears,
The echoes linger, fade with fears.
With every farewell whispered low,
The voyager's spirit starts to glow.

The Silent Call of Approaching Shadows

Beneath the veil of twilight's sigh,
The shadows dance, they drift and fly.
They're whispers from a time long past,
Layers of secrets that ever last.

In the murmurs of the fading light,
A silent call invites the night.
With every heartbeat, time unfolds,
The tales of warmth, of courage bold.

As darkness wraps the earth in grace,
The shadows gather, find their place.
In stillness deep, the world suspends,
Where echoes loom, and silence bends.

Embrace the night, the calm that stays,
In shadows' hold, the heart replayed.
A calling felt in the quiet throng,
Where every shadow sings its song.

The Train That Knew No Destination

A whistle blows, the engine roars,
It travels forth to distant shores.
Through landscapes vast, both wild and free,
The train moves on with mystery.

No ticket bought, no course defined,
The journey's song, a twist entwined.
Through tunnels dark and valleys wide,
Each moment feels like a joyous ride.

The trees rush past, a blurred embrace,
While strangers share a fleeting space.
Together bound by rails of fate,
Their stories merge, they contemplate.

But when the sun begins to set,
The wanderers know there's no regret.
For in the journey, life is found,
The train of dreams, it goes around.

Journeys Woven in Twilight Tales

The sky ignites in hues of gold,
While tales of twilight softly unfold.
In the hush of dusk, secrets bloom,
Voices carry where shadows loom.

Each story spun from threads of night,
Woven with laughter, woven with fright.
In journeys shared by the fire's glow,
Hearts entwine as the embers flow.

With every heartbeat, memories weave,
Enchanted tales that we believe.
Through winding paths and starlit skies,
A tapestry forms before our eyes.

In twilight's arms, we find our peace,
A tapestry rich that won't decrease.
For in these tales, we forever dwell,
In journeys woven, our hearts do swell.

Riddles on Rails

Beneath the stars, the iron twists,
Whispers of journeys, the night insists.
Tracks of shadows, secrets concealed,
A puzzle of paths, fate revealed.

Each station a tale, a fleeting glance,
Fragments of stories, lost in dance.
Who rides the car with a heavy heart?
The rail's gentle sigh, a work of art.

Wheels turning soft on gravel and steel,
Echoes of laughter, the past they steal.
In silence they speak, the riddle unfolds,
A journey of whispers, the truth it holds.

Through tunnels of darkness, light breaks anew,
Endless horizons, a world to view.
So heed the call of the train in the night,
For riddles on rails can spark the light.

Mystique in Motion

Windswept whispers race through the trees,
Moonlight beckons with gentle ease.
Footfalls hidden, yet beckoning still,
Each breath a promise, a heart to thrill.

The dance of shadows, a fleeting glance,
Twilight's embrace in a ghostly trance.
Voices echo where secrets abide,
In dreams entwined, the dark will guide.

Mystery drapes like a velvet shawl,
Softly it beckons, inviting us all.
Time shimmers, bends in the gentle night,
With every heartbeat, mystery takes flight.

So follow the whispers, let silence sway,
Through corridors where the lost shall play.
In motion they drift, like smoke in the air,
Mystique and wonder, forever to share.

The Unseen Traveler's Tale

In the shadows, a figure roams,
Cloaked in whispers, away from homes.
Footsteps echo on cobblestones bare,
Stories wrapped in the midnight air.

With eyes like lanterns, they search the night,
Each corner a puzzle, a flickering light.
Histories linger where silence unfolds,
The unseen traveler spins tales untold.

Paths intertwine where destinies cross,
A moment shared, yet nothing is lost.
Specters of memories dance in the mist,
A ghostly embrace, a lover's tryst.

For those who wander, the unseen awaits,
In alleyways dark, through time's heavy gates.
So heed the shadows, let the journey unfurl,
The unseen traveler, a whispering swirl.

Departure of the Unknown

A train on the tracks, a rumble within,
Hearts beat in sync as the journey begins.
Whistles and steam, a powerful call,
The unknown awaits, we answer its thrall.

Glimpses of landscapes whiz past our eyes,
Each station a chapter, a new surprise.
With tickets in hand, we board with a sigh,
Embracing the moments, the lows and the high.

Trains carry dreams on their iron backs,
Voyagers gathering, filling the tracks.
As cultures collide in a rush of the new,
The departure of unknown, a vibrant hue.

So onward we travel, with stories to weave,
Into the horizon, our hearts on our sleeves.
In every farewell, a promise to heed,
The departure of unknown, where we're meant to lead.

The Lurking Passenger

In shadowed corners, eyes do gleam,
A figure whispers, lost in dream.
Breathless silence, secrets shared,
On the train where none have dared.

Fingers linger on the seat,
Hearts quicken with each heartbeat.
A smile creeps, though none can see,
The lurking passenger's mystery.

Through the tunnel, echoes call,
Voices soft, then silence falls.
With every stop, we all might find,
A passenger left far behind.

The door swings wide, a fleeting glance,
Is it fate or just a chance?
As shadows dance and lights do play,
The looming truth fades far away.

Twilight Tales of the Twilight Train

In twilight's clutch, the train rolls on,
Stories weave with fading dawn.
Passengers glance, their tales untold,
In whispered words, their lives unfold.

A mother hums a lonesome tune,
While lovers sigh beneath the moon.
Memories dance in twilight's embrace,
Each face a map, each smile a trace.

The ticket clerk with weary eyes,
Recalls the dreams of silent skies.
Every journey holds a key,
Unlocking hearts, setting them free.

As night descends, the lanterns glow,
Guiding souls the way to go.
With every stop, new tales arise,
As twilight whispers, the heart complies.

Voyages into the Unknown

Upon the rails, adventures spark,
To distant lands, to journeys stark.
The whistle blows, the engines roar,
What waits beyond that distant shore?

Curious minds peer through the glass,
To fleeting sights that come and pass.
With every mile, the questions grow,
What wonders lie, what fears bestow?

Train cars hum with vibrant life,
Strangers bond, share joy and strife.
They dream of lands where dreams come true,
Where skies are vast, and hopes renew.

As stars appear, the night unfolds,
In silent whispers, courage molds.
Each voyage taken, a chance to find,
The magic world within the mind.

Whimsical Travels in Darkened Avenues

Down avenues where shadows play,
The midnight train steals dreams away.
In whimsical arcs, the journey bends,
Through streets of night where laughter blends.

With lanterns bright, the path aglow,
Each corner turned, new wonders show.
Mysterious stores with treasures rare,
Invite the dreamers, those who dare.

A jester grins, he winks and bows,
While clocks tick soft, beneath the sows.
The magic swells in every heartbeat,
Whimsical tunes, our minds repeat.

So take a ride with hearts alight,
Embrace the joy, the whimsical night.
For in these travels, lost we'll find,
The dreams we seek, our hearts entwined.

Tales from the Twilight Carriages

Whispers echo in dusk's gentle embrace,
Stories linger where shadows find space.
Carriages creak on tracks worn and thin,
Ancient tales where journeys begin.

Hearts collide in the warmth of the night,
Flickering lanterns cast a soft light.
Each passenger holds a dream in their hand,
As twilight envelops this magic land.

Conversations dance like fireflies' flight,
In this fleeting world, time feels just right.
Memories shared will forever remain,
In whispers of love, joy, and pain.

So travel these rails with an open heart,
Discover the beauty in every part.
For twilight carriages hold more than they claim,
Each ride is a journey, never the same.

Puzzles in the Station's Silence

In the quiet hum of the waiting hall,
Time stands still, as shadows fall.
Empty benches hold stories untold,
Puzzles of lives, both meek and bold.

Footsteps echo on the polished stone,
Each sound a reminder we're not alone.
Faces blur in the dimly lit space,
Seeking solace, or perhaps a trace.

Whispers of travelers, hopes set aflame,
Every farewell, every name.
The clock ticks on, with secrets it keeps,
In the still of the night, the station sleeps.

Yet within this silence, a spell is spun,
Connection flows, two hearts become one.
For every puzzle that time may splice,
In gathering moments, we find our slice.

Tracks of the Unmarked Path

On the edge where wildflowers bloom,
Lie tracks leading to endless room.
Paths uncharted by man's strong hand,
Whispering dreams of a secret land.

Footsteps falter, yet spirits soar,
Each bend revealing an unseen door.
Nature embraces with every breath,
Guiding us close to the edge of death.

In the quiet thrum of the forest's heart,
Lies a wisdom that won't depart.
Listen closely to the rhythms of life,
Feel the pulse beyond worldly strife.

For tracks unmarked hold stories anew,
Each step a dance, each glance a view.
In the wild we find solace and grace,
On unmarked paths, we embrace our place.

The Tapestry of Travel and Time

Threads of moments weave through the air,
Where travel unfurls without a care.
Every mile, a stitch in the grand design,
Crafting a story that forever will shine.

From bustling cities to quiet retreats,
Each journey begins where the heartbeat meets.
Maps of the soul drawn with a fine brush,
In the dance of adventure, we feel the rush.

Connection forms in the fleeting glance,
Cultures intertwining in a sacred dance.
Every step a note in the song of the earth,
Celebrating life, connection, and birth.

So travel onward with open eyes,
Embrace each moment as it swiftly flies.
In the tapestry woven with care and rhyme,
We find our place in the fabric of time.

Tracks that Lead to Nowhere

Rusty rails beneath my feet,
Whispers of a past so sweet.
Echoes of footsteps long gone,
In shadowed paths, I wander on.

Overgrown weeds mark the way,
Dreams of travel, led astray.
Sunsets fade in hues of gold,
While stories of old tales unfold.

The journey starts but never ends,
Where every curve the mind bends.
Lost horizons call my name,
In this dance, I feel no shame.

A train of thought on vacant tracks,
Chasing whispers, no looking back.
Through tangled dreams, I roam free,
Where time's embrace won't capture me.

The Puzzle of the Endless Journey

Pieces scattered, paths entwined,
A journey mapped but undefined.
Each turn a riddle yet to solve,
In the chaos, worlds evolve.

Stepping stones on shifting sand,
A compass held in trembling hand.
Questions linger in the air,
Each heartbeat leads me somewhere.

Clouds above a canvas bright,
Colors blend in fading light.
Every motion brings me near,
To truths I've hidden out of fear.

Moments captured, fleeting fast,
A moving train, a shadow cast.
In the puzzle, I will find,
The pieces of a heart aligned.

Enigmatic Encounters at Twilight

In twilight's glow, the world suspends,
Whispers dance where daylight ends.
Figures flicker, shapes unfold,
Secrets shared in hues of gold.

Silent gazes, stories told,
In enigmatic folds, unfold.
Memories woven in twilight's thread,
Of journeys taken, paths we're led.

A fleeting smile, a lingering sigh,
Moments that spark, then say goodbye.
Underneath the crescent moon,
Time slips by, a hushed tune.

Within the dusk, connections spark,
In every shadow, every arc.
Twilight's grip, a moment shared,
In the quiet, hearts are bared.

Aboard the Mystery Locomotive

Chugging softly down the track,
A whispering steam, no looking back.
Windows fogged with tales untold,
Adventures wait, brave and bold.

Midnight rides through valleys deep,
Where secrets of the night will seep.
Carriages echo with distant dreams,
In twilight's arms, nothing's as it seems.

Ticket stubs of memories past,
Each stop a chance, each journey vast.
Aboard this train of chance and fate,
I meet the unknown; I take my place.

Through misty nights and starry skies,
With every turn, the heart sighs.
The mystery flows, a river wide,
Onward through time, I'm swept with pride.

Milton Keynes UK
Ingram Content Group UK Ltd.
UKHW021128021124
450571UK00005B/76

9 789916 903148